Happy Tears
&
Rainbow Babies

Written by: Natasha Melissa Carlow

Illustrated by: Keevyn Mohammed and Kyle Stephen

For Kyleigh Rose, and Caspian, my precious rainbow babies. I love you with all my heart.

For Kylelan, the love of my life and my number one supporter. I am so grateful for you.

For Pops, who never stopped believing.

For Jarett and Jaxn, and Rainbow Babies everywhere.

Copyright © 2019 by Natasha Carlow
Happy Tears and Rainbow Babies
Library of Congress Control Number: 2018964364
ISBN: 978-1-948604-20-8
Illustrations by
Design by Heidi Schweigert, heidischweigert.com
Purple Butterfly Press, katbiggiepress.com
Printed in the United States of America
All Rights Reserved.

PURPLE BUTTERFLY PRESS
katbiggiepress.com

Rosie and Capi looked at each other
and giggled with glee.
They were going for a walk
with Mommy and Daddy. This was
their most favourite thing to do.

At five years old,
Rosie was already the
best big sister a brother
could ask for.

She helped Mommy put on her little brother's shoes
and hat and he rewarded her
with a huge, sloppy kiss on the cheek.

She threw her head back
and laughed
and pretended to run away.

Daddy lifted Capi up into his arms
and Rosie grabbed mommy's
outstretched hand. It was time to go.

As they set off on their walk,
Mommy and Daddy pointed out
all their usual sights.

They waved hello to Mr Greg,
the neighbour with the beautiful
flowers growing in his yard.

They barked at Peaches
the little brown dog
who lived down the street.

As Peaches barked back and
wiggled his tail with glee,
Rosie and Capi wiggled their
bodies pretending to have
a tail just like Peaches.

This made Daddy and Mommy laugh
every time. Rosie and Capi loved
hearing Mommy and Daddy laugh.

One of their favourite stops on their walk was the little park with the pond full of fish. As they approached the park Rosie pulled on Mommy's hand and took off running and Capi motioned to go down.

Daddy carefully set him down and he wobbled off after his sister. He was only three years old but he already loved copying everything she did.

Soon they were at their favourite spot,
the little pond. Mommy set the blanket down
and they settled down on it to have a snack.

Rosie stuffed her mouth full with grapes
and Capi dipped his hand in his yogurt, licking
it off his fingers. Suddenly Rosie cried out,
"Mommy look! It's a rainbow!"

Capi clapped his hands and cried,
" Rain-bow rain-bow."
Mommy and Daddy looked at
the rainbow and smiled at each
other, as a tiny tear rolled down
Mommy's cheek.

"Oh no, Mommy, don't cry!"
Rosie exclaimed as she crawled
over unto Mommy's lap.
"Don't you like rainbows?"

"Oh sweetheart,
I love rainbows,
in fact these
are happy tears."
"What are happy tears?"
Rosie asked.

"Well," said Daddy, "sometimes when mommy
gets very happy, she just can't contain
all the happiness inside, so a little bit spills
out in the shape of a tear."

"Oh like when I pour too much juice in my
sippy cup and some spills out?" Rosie asked.

"Exactly!" Mommy and Daddy said and laughed in unison. Rosie continued eating her snack and Capi pulled out his toy cars and began driving them up and down Daddy's back.

After a few minutes,
Rosie turned to mommy
and asked,

"Mommy, I like rainbows,
but not enough to spill
out my happiness,
why do you love
rainbows so much?"

Mommy pulled Rosie closer and gave her a big hug
and a kiss and patted Capi lovingly on the head.

"Well, first rainbows are beautiful to look at,
don't you agree?" Rosie and Capi nodded.
"But also, rainbows remind me of just how much
God loves me. You see a long time ago, God put
the first rainbow in the sky as a promise between
Himself and the people who lived then…"

"Like in the story of Noah?"
Rosie interrupted excitedly.

"Yes, exactly like in the story of Noah."
Daddy responded and smiled.

"But did you know the rainbow can also be used to mean something else?" He asked.

"A rainbow is also a symbol that many families have used to represent something beautiful and meaningful.

The rainbow is also a symbol for families, like us, who have had to say goodbye to babies before they could be born, but then went on to welcome more babies into their family.

These new babies are
called Rainbow Babies."
Rosie looked at Capi,
who stared back
and sneezed.

"Let me try," Mommy said laughing.

"You know that you and Capi were in my tummy and then Mommy gave birth to you, right? Well, before you were born, Daddy and I had other babies in my tummy, but those babies never made it to being born.

That was a very sad time for Daddy and me, but we believe that God loved us, so we continued to pray and eventually God gave us you and Capi.

That's what Daddy meant by we had to say goodbye to other babies before we had you and your brother."

"I think I understand a little bit." Rosie said.
"I know it can be confusing, but we love you and Capi very much and we are here to answer any questions you have," Daddy said.

"Ummm, do you still feel sad that the babies weren't born?" Rosie asked.

"Sometimes I do," Mommy said nodding, "but every time I see a rainbow it reminds me of those babies and that God still gave us two beautiful babies to be parents to."

"I just wish I could see them and play with them," Rosie cried, snuggling closer to Mommy's chest.

"It's okay to be a little sad. It's always hard when someone we love dies, but even though we can't see them or touch them, we can do things to remember them with love every day. For me, I try to be the best husband and father by praying for you all every day," Daddy said.

"And I try to always tell you both and show you how much you are loved and how grateful I am to have all of you. And maybe later we can do a special project to help you and Capi remember them." Mommy said.

Capi jumped up to chase after a butterfly, and Rosie looked away thoughtfully. After a few minutes she said, "So Capi and I are Rainbow babies?"

When Mommy nodded she continued. "You know what I think? I think that a rainbow baby is kind of a promise, just like the other rainbow and I am so happy that Capi and I get to remind you of how much God loves and cares for our family.

Also I think that you are the best Mommy and Daddy Capi and I could ever have and tonight when we say our bedtime prayers I will remember to thank God for our family, especially our brothers and sisters who are with Him."

This time, there were tears in both Mommy and Daddy's eyes.